Praise for *So*

C000040557

"*If Kerouac had been a better poet he would have written like William R. Soldan. They both cover some of the same territory, geographically and philosophically, only Soldan has remembered to pack his heart and his perceptions for the road, sees both the humor and edges of these rough days, and presents them in lines that will echo in our minds for a lifetime.*"

> — **Mindi Kirchner**, author of *Song of the Rest of Us* and *The Law of Almosts*

"*Stark, honest, and of the earth, the poems in So Fast, So Close stab at the heart, 'choking you as you grope in the dark.' From the first poem in the collection to the last, Soldan never fails to risk hope through characters who are too drunk to sing, who can chew through a beer can, or a bus that never takes you to your destination though it 'arrives each time to take you there.' With every line, every turn of phrase, we are exalted by a candid, concrete lyricism. And by the end we trust unquestionably the poet's reassurance that there is refuge in illimitable uncertainty, beauty in the wonderous and fragmentary.*"

> — **Ralph Pennel**, Editor, *Midway Journal*

So Fast,
So Close

by

William R. Soldan

Close To The Bone Publishing

Close To The Bone

Rugby

Warwickshire

United Kingdom

CV21

www.close2thebone.co.uk

Interior Design by Craig Douglas

Cover by Craig Douglas

First Printing, 2020

Contents

◆

3

Fathers and Sons

For my father and my only son

1

Roads and Cities

Greyhound

Not the planes you took solo some summers
to see your grandma, your father's blood.
Not the Amtrak you took with your mother in
dark-of-morning rain to pick up a set of wheels to
get you through winter. But the bus bounding
three days westward. Watching lives, landscapes,
shaping and shrinking like moments: exchanges in stations,
the French woman who sat beside you, offered you gum
in her sweet tongue as you puffed an unlit Camel in OK City,
just blocks away from buildings scarred by the bomb.
The one you rode north, tracking miles through gray plains,
drinking masked brandy, sharing blankets with strangers
while your wife was getting clean back east.
The one that never reached your destination
but arrived each time to take you there.

Layover

The Whistle Stop Inn—

as if this were some brick and wrought iron lodging
on the cobbled street of a foggy gas-lit square
instead of a dive bar across from a Hoosier state bus terminal.
But what are names but falsehoods anyway,
a drink but a way to kill time?
And if dollars were bullets, buddy, I'd have enough slugs
to pick off the lonely minutes until bodies of hours lay in heaps
all along this cold dead street.
My hands are stiff and splintered from loading and unloading
trucks to get this far (and yet only halfway there),
with cash that's lasted longer than it ever would have
now that the monkey's been sent packing.
Sure, it'll be gone before too long, too soon not to toast those still
standing
or falling or lying prone with hands splayed and reaching out,
those closing the place down or huddled beside the station doors,
spare-changing to cop a shot or a half-pint bottle
like those on the shelf above the till.
So let's do this right and finish it off, all of it, what we started
since departing, all that's left before we go.

Upper Peninsula

After a week in the deep
north woods, pitched in a bog
staked with quaking aspen,
a week of fire and rainbows
and midnight spirits,
the shore of this body,
rocky maw of a great blue wolf,
spreads out beside us at a highway clip,
sun dipping red like a dripping
wound.
And what a sight it is.
What a place to pull off,
to sink fingers into shell-sharp sand
and close them around a moment,
lift it, let it sift and ripple,
the first fist of dirt
on another day interred.

Border Crossing

Dark by the time we stopped
but now a morning view of vastness
and valleys,
bear cubs scavenging the trash
of travelers like us.

People snapping pictures
while their kids get too close.

It's best to smoke the last of the stash,
leave the pipes and papers
as offerings to those
returning.

We load up on cartons of cigarettes
at the Duty Free, then drive up the road,
where a guy hands them off to us
like some illicit package about a mile
from the Canadian border.

There, they keep us for hours
but are so polite as they unpack the van
that by the end it's almost hard to hold
a grudge.

Once back into the green-hung timber
we stop to watch a black bear barrel
down a dirt road.
One of our number pulls a joint from the
sole of his shoe, says, *Got a light?*

I could break his teeth
but hug him instead.

Kenora

Here the gloaming sky is like those old
    but now long cold Ohio hearths
        in their days and nights of belching fire,

the water red and rippling like liquid steel.
    But it is decades from that false promise
        and many miles from all that rust, the place we left to

when the fractures deepened past the point of mending,
    closer it is to where we started, the city by the lake
        that remains the biggest part of him I carry

besides his name.
    This would be his heaven, *lac des bois*, with its winding
        shore and dark depths.

I can almost see him if I try, casting from this dock
    or trolling out above the shoals as loons let loose
        their thin-throated sorrows better than we ever could.

Winnipeg

We were only a few months into this,
us, this thing we have, when her uncle
wrapped his hand around mine like a vise
only doing what it was made for
and said, *Welcome to the family.*
I listened for the unspoken note beneath it,
the one that had trailed every first love since
the second grade,
but then they pulled me into the fold and
slapped my back.
I waited.

And now, these men talking of hockey and horses
instead of dope and prison.
Celluloid negatives of the ones
that live in my strands, whom I've only ever known
in faded snapshots and bygone summers,
but who emerge at the worst of times.

At the Opium we drink, and I speak with that lilt of
drawn out vowels and slightly upturned phrases,
all in good humor till I can't stop myself.
I gauge the reaction of the bartender, who's been kicking
us every couple on the house because the night is young
and the house is dead. He's a good sport.

My old man's from Wisconsin. Got family there.
You all remind me of them,
only less pissed off all the time, ya knooow?

Out on the street, a man and woman, First Nations,
share their curb with us and we croon together, he and I,

and I think, Who am I to feel displaced?
The woman keeps telling the woman I love she loves her style,
and the woman I love gives the woman her skirt,
and this gesture is just part of why I love her.
The woman cries, and they spin in circles.
The man and I share drinks from a bottle of Kokanee beer.
What we speak of is anyone's guess and matters little.
He chants at the moon, and I listen.
In case this is the rest of our life.
In case this is all there is.

Back in the States

At the border, they take drills to our doors,
everything short of greasing up a rubber glove.
The mosquitoes are ferocious, drink their fill
as we plow south down potted two-lane,
a buzzing cloud seething around the cab, our things—
books, clothes, trinkets made or traded for—tossed
by careless hands.

The road parts the sleeping grassland country like
a zipper or an unstitched seam, body around it
soaked in moon glow, the ridge and hollow of a hip
or the slope of soft shoulder spied through a midnight curtain.

Then he hits a fox at fifty-five, and we spend an hour
in a field, among the sway, believing it's still alive.
His spirit animal, or someone else's.

*Some believe that to see a fox at the start of a journey
is a bad omen*, he says.

But we've been out here for many weeks now,
and besides, it's dying, even dead.

But they're said to inspire swiftness of mind and body, too,
he says, and shrugs.

So what does any of it mean, I ask, *if everything means anything*?

They're most active in the night, he says.

We never find it, not even its trail.
We drive until we find the sun,
or it finds us.

Missoula

1.

Rolled in late and slept beside a Taco Bell, woke up
dried out and soaked, gasping with the windows closed.

First coffee, then our sense of direction, looking for labor,
meet a trio hoofing off a main drag, tell them to tag along,
soon headed west to that city of rain.

But then a cold case and respite on the brambled bank,
a patchwork gaggle passing-through from every point:
kid from New York going to or coming from,
can't hold still to tell the tale, and some woman calling herself
Iron Butterfly, maternal with sandwiches and soup, passing around
papers and a pouch of moist shag. A Scorpio named Cula singing
Inna-Gadda-Da-Vida Baby like some primitive mating call.

Later, a guy named Doc with knotted locks knocks out
a dude named Buddha, makes him bleed beneath a sliver of summer
moon,
while a girl with a drum hangs upside down by her knees in a tree,
laughing.

His farewell bid alliterates
in the distant hills:

Best 'member me, Muthafucka.

2.

Wake in a field of flattened grass, bodies sprawled
around smoldering ash, the sun searing its arc toward midday.

Someone says, *Shit*, then, *C'mon*, then, *Hurry*.

Seattle

1.

He said he's trying to get home to see his boy,
knows the city like he knows loss, and brother,
he's lost it all.

Spire on the horizon, retro-futurist
palace in pink clouds.

Looking for life on a Broadway strip but finding
a thousand kinds of death dressed in rags
with bags on their backs and chemical eyes.

Cop a sack of glass from a kid with a can
with a false bottom, blast off beside a dumpster,
break the shackles of gravity—

pinging   blips on a radar screen
                above roads   skipping scenes
            the voices singing
                    bodies
                        human percussion of
                crashing   atoms
                    in parks and alleys
                in the wide open
            stalking sidewalks
        for a place to set up
            a place to trade these songs
                for silver
            our collision of limbs
        stripped fingers grieving snapped
    E and G strings   pulling notes from on high or low

15

to fill the spaces till   coins pile into wine
    and faces   places led and followed to   erratic procession
        each car riding   deep   to where the street meets water
           lights like drowning stars

2.

How many hours has it been, how many days
How many warm beers in paper cups to keep low
How many trips to the bathroom in the park
How many needle caps and nickel Zip-locs like bread crumbs left by
would-be lost children
How long before the rain
How many dudes with schemes looking for a wheel-man
How man runaways for a way out, turned away because of the heat
they'd bring despite these cold dawns
How many faces and names, how many bodies have we fostered and
shed like so much weight

3.

The rare days, rainless and clear,
now sheer with mist like white nylon.
Everything an image from a dream
we're driving out of.
We get him home or the place he claims,
idle at the curb as he knuckles the door.
It opens and shuts and he hangs his head.
We drop him on the southbound
before we go north.
It's the least we can do, I tell him,
after all we've been through.

Reno

The Biggest Little City in the World, but tonight
just another dour oasis no different than the last.
Had family out here, gave up north snow for glitz
and blasted sands. Twelve, thirteen years old when
he called collect from a Nevada slam. Years before
he told me why: he'd robbed a casino—the Atlantis
or Peppermill, or maybe the Grand Sierra—that
I was his *neph* and he loved me like a son.

His sister was out here running, too, keeping Johns to
keep atop a mean jones. Or was it Phoenix or Santa Fe?
Bought me smokes and a cold sixer, took me to a trailer
party in the Wisconsin woods last time I saw her. She'd
had a husband who ate a twelve-gauge slug and left nothing
but a ghost and red memory. Imagine that'd twist a person
a dozen different ways.

I see them the way they were, hell-bent and a hundred feet tall.
We swore he'd outlive us all, but weren't surprised when he didn't.
Though I wonder if she's here, among these tired faces, beneath
these greasy lights, or elsewhere on the basin, perhaps calling
along the many faults for someone to bring her home, even far as
Badwater, sinking into the salt.

Flagstaff

"They say he's wanted in like three states..." -**Rainbow kid**

On a blanket in the grass
a man named Gypsy and his band

of followers, children,
bartering toward the next forest,

next nowhere.
A handful of faux chevron beads

for a silver-wrapped moonstone,
his eyes like chips of prism crystal

in the shadow of a brown suede hat.
Come on along. Always room for more.

The sun setting behind the mountains,
the night we leave.

For us, the unknown stops here,
in this city of strange weather.

A peyote stitch,
a strand of blown-glass teardrops.

Seven dollars and a
three-finger pinch of tobacco.

The last glance
a mossy smile and a nod.

Happy travels.
Keep it breezy.

Then, down the road, we hear they were
putting people in the soup,

doled out at gatherings.
Still out there, moving,

bellies full,
numbers growing,

shrinking,
trading trinkets for fuel.

Hellmouth in the High Desert, a Dervish

after Steven Reese

We'd be hard-pressed to find
a more storied departure than setting out
from an Ohio forge, long quenched and rusty in spite
of a city's thirst,
    to another, trekking the sparse,
        flat vasculature of Kansas
    through towns as cast off as jetsam
and not even spotted
    on the trusty Rand McNally,
        this ocean dust-choked, blued only by the blur
    of distance,
through Dodge City,
"Where Wyatt Earp never set a single dang foot,"
according to some old codger or another;

and the farther we get
to where the sun sinks belly-up,
to not think of those we've succeeded,
    who hoofed and wagon-wheeled their trails,
        and wonder how many revisions they made
    as they conquered this great sage frontier;
to find a straight line to the past on the page,
    the roots of our legends,
        the stories deciphered then told
    then etched in pulp, as the stone glyphs
on this New Mexican ruin of the vanished
Anasazi, this *Urraca Mesa*, where in lieu
of Cerberus,

cats seal and stand guard against
    all manner of hell.

The voice in the air here is all manner, too,
whether it's the Navajo shaman who still
    roams the slopes cloaked in blue light,
        or some quiver-backed Apache,
    or the resurrection of a lone warrior,
returned to keep watch;
    versions as far off as a lost scout led astray
        by a frenzied needle
    to the headless corpse of Black Jack Ketchum,
that old outlaw,
    popping his pistols
        with a jig and a *yee-haw*!

So which rendition of the
divine vestibule awaits
beyond the mouth but before the gullet?
    Perhaps the portent of the magpie,
        chatterbox harbinger of ill matters;
    or just a simple carving in the arch:
Abandon all hope, ye who
    hear it call;
        perhaps it's
    nothing at all.

Science has it lodestone
    draws the lightning,
        buggers the compass,
    but who's to say, really,
which iteration is mere myth,
    any more than our whirling westward

        in search of something?

In the Shadow of Circling Birds

I've had this fantasy since I was young:
coming to a place like this, like so many
passed through to get here, lancscape hazed
with heat and spirits, towns like the scattered toys
of some bored Titan, left to warp and rust beneath
a raging star, in wind of dust, in fugitive rain,
to drink fire and the blood of snakes in the curtained
rooms of shoebox motels till dusk, when I'd stumble
booted and whiskey drunk, tumble into the brush of
a whispering arroyo, eyes to the glittering wheel, which
would slowly dim and wink out when the sun took its turn,
plenty of light for the vultures picking at my bones.

Amarillo

O bastard Spanish Rose,
Land of black-tailed jacks and rattlesnake plains,
nodding derricks and tombstone Cadillacs, of nukes,
set at the western end of that windy alley, where the finger of God
can show mercy or destroy, where throughout the Llano Estacado
and Palo Duro, Hoodoo rocks aim like arrows at the sun.

Where along what was once the Mother Road,
banked by dusty scrub and red earth,
one can rest and be regaled with tales of extraordinary men,
who came and conquered: of the Klondike Bills and Bunky Millers,
of Frank Pastore, that Red from Cincinnati, who died on a
motorcycle,
but not before rising the victor.

What they don't tell you at a distance, some will say,
is you gotta finish the whole mess.
As did Hoss Dearduff and Digger Jones.
As did Fat Boy Honinsworth, Bodie Freeman, and Memphis Black.
Dickie Van Der Snel.
Beefmaster Huggins.
A man with such a grand constitution they dubbed him A-Team.
Every last scrap. That's where they getcha.

Yet not even two-time champion Bear Dog Hoffman,
or three-timer Eli Ghattas, had what it took
to take down the likes of Molly Schuyler, one hundred twenty-four
pound lass, who ate not one, but two 72 ouncers in a single sitting,
who defied the odds, the fates, annihilated an entire flank,
masticated crisp leaves and shrimp and buttered bread,
a tater the size of a newborn babe.

23

For what is this if not a land of great triumph, of everything larger
than life,
as is proclaimed in the songs of the age, emblazoned on the gaudy
armor,
signaled in the rifle crack of that proud Lonestar standard?

Though as we hear of these heroes, let us remember
those that came and went without a name, who,
for every Achilles and Heracles, for every solitary Goddess,
surged in droves, but are so often forgotten, as if they had never lived.

Cheyenne

A between hour between things,
dark night of the soul hour,

hour of the wolf.
A van rambling bald Bridgestones

through unseen prairies,
static stringing broken blues

and cracked, early morning *hallelujahs.*

East toward central time,
time-travelling on land,

cash-wise tapped, coins
and a few wrinkled bills,

sunk and hungry, tank burning miles,
miles gone and miles calling.

No condition.
For any of this, sleepless.

Almost Christmas and the world
is brown and brow beaten

ghosts coast into gravel and
neon light.

A bite, a steaming cup
before they go bust.

Street Kid's Guide to Coming up Aces in Columbus, Ohio

Key to making it's this: First, just let go. Especially in warmer months—May through September things really open up. Winter gets tricky, but there's always head west or south. If you're really desperate, borrow an address, some digits, get a job till things thaw out. Only if you're desperate, understand. Next thing's knowing Jimmy John's offs their day-old bread for fifty cents, a little over three cents an inch, so jump on it. Ain't tough to come up with a couple quarters, and bread'll keep you going a long time. Then hit up the UDF dumpsters on High, usually good for a sixer or two of expired brew. Bread, brew, guy's got practically everything he needs. Smokes—strangers are good for one on the street, but posting up outside the Shell station or the Sunoco on Hudson is how you do it. Most dudes oblige when you catch 'em peeling the strip off a fresh pack. When all else fails, the snipes in the ashtray sand outside B-Dubs are some of the longest in town, if you don't mind sucking on someone else's filter—and for real if you've already hit the needle (come on, ain't no one judging you here), then what's a couple germs in the grand scheme? Oh, and there's those Micky D's coupons sold in those little booklets in the summertime: ten sundaes for two bucks—and nothing like a spoonful of cool cream on a hot day. That's the gist. Just remember spare changing's an art. So bring it. Spit some lines. Pick a tune. Shit, hit a lick with a grift if it's in you. If you got the steady hands and can keep straight the bent truths. Finally, you'll need a place to sleep when coming down from running hard (because that's what we do), a few hours to reset or a whole day through. And in a town like this, for real, there's always somebody.

2

So Fast, So Close

Always that Child

It has become so important that you not forget that you quickly slip into the present tense. You were not that child. Always are and never were. As if remembering what can hardly be put into words will somehow prove (to whom?) you existed at all. Ex*ist* at all.

Screams heard from the waiting room, not yours—you don't hear yours—but hers as she pushes someone else into this world. You've not long known yourself and don't know that you don't know, and won't. Even when you do.

The First Sign, 1988

Your kindergarten teacher starts sending you home with daily reports because you've been acting out. Disobeying. Being yourself.

You don't know who else to be.

A scale from one to five: Fours and fives mean no discomfort but what you feel inside; ones and twos mean the hand, the corner, the empty stomach; threes—threes are a gamble.

Your big sister—half sister—tries to help you prepare, holds the envelope up to the sun so that you might know your fate. But you never quite know, do you? And that much won't change, even when so much does. This ritual will be the one by which you gauge so many things.

An envelope sealed tight, held against a blinding light.

Like Yesterday

A young girl blinds you with a handful of sand as you play in the park, and you will one day wonder why you remember this so clearly.

Another metric, perhaps. Another metaphor.

So many spend their lives searching for just the right one.

And here it is. Sand in your face, your mouth, choking you as you grope in the dark.

No Grand Departure

Before you've had the chance to grow into anything it's time to go.

Your mother has an apartment sale. *We need the money*, she says. *To get where we're goin'. And we just don't have the room.*

So you watch as strangers enter and leave and enter and leave, making low-ball offers and taking things, the twinkle of coins and the rasp of a few small bills telling you already what your life is worth.

The room you shared with your brother emptied, all but what can fit in the car. Not much. A small car. And your brother, gone. Your sister. And this home is not your home.

Past, Present, Future

You move in with a friend of hers. A peeling foursquare on a blind street overlooking the interstate. A man from her past. Before you. He has several large dogs and carries a gun under his left arm.

The city looks bombed out, cracked bricks and falling down buildings, mills ten years gone but still standing in the gash of low ground that cuts through the heart of it all.

You have to walk to the end of the block to catch the school bus. Sometimes your mom walks with you and bums cigarettes from the older kids hanging out behind the corner store with the grated windows and neon sign. She didn't smoke. But now she does.

It will be many years before you find out that she tried to join the military shortly before you left to come here. They wouldn't take her. Years before you wonder what exactly that would have meant, for you.

Water off a Broken Wing

Seven years old and you have your own house key. You know how to cook your own dinner. Most of the time she leaves you something to just heat up, but sometimes—

Nothing you can't handle.

Just like you handle the unease daily. Of walking to school from another new place in another bad neighborhood, worse even than the last: kids on the news every night, shot dead over jackets and shoes.

Someday your wife will say, *That wasn't a thing that really happened*, and you'll try not to point out her privilege when you say, *It was a thing. Happened every day.* You'll tell her to look it up, and she'll look it up and see and apologize. *Why would I lie?* you'll say. *I just thought—What? It's just, you know how people exaggerate.* Your love will understand, but your life lived will make it hard.

After the Hands

You have no history, none that you know of. One day you will wish to explore the absence, but want for a road through it. Part of you will feel robbed. Part of you will be too busy getting by to care.

You look for signs of connection. Between yourself and yourself. Yourself and this disarticulated life. Severed. You know them when you see them. But sometimes you don't.

You find one in a line in a book. Others in broken things.

Your mother works herself into a new hip and is still on her feet. Emptying trash and vacuuming floors. Cleaning people's shit from bathroom stalls. Invisible. She eats her lunch on the move because there's just never enough time. She chases it with pain pills she can't afford because she can't afford to stop.

The metal in her leg makes her ache. Her back aches. Her hands. So stiff and inflamed she can hardly make a fist to shake at the sky. And when the hands go, what then? You're sure she wonders as much as you, but she doesn't complain. Just keeps moving.

Before She Stopped Living

after Nin Andrews

She stopped wearing her wig, and it reminded you of the times you would pass her bedroom door, cracked enough to see her sleeping, gray strands unpinned, laying long and limp on the pillow. At that age you felt the fear that there was some stranger, a weathered crone asleep in her bed, skin fissured like a slab of old stone. Each time you would run away, and each time she would step through that same door, black curls you thought were her own, tight as inky springs, beehived above her, and you would sneak a peek, and the stranger would be gone.

Mom helped out most with the little things: getting her tissues and water and pills, propping her up. Wiping her down, reading her the paper. She was there out of duty, not love. She did not love her, had said so many times. *I have nothing but hatred for that woman.* You helped carry her to the car when she was moved to hospice. She wore the wig then, and lipstick and powder. The smell of her dying beneath it, as if it knew it had finished what it had come to do and now was leaking out, looking for something else to blacken. You kissed her cheek, already cold and tacky like wet dough, because she asked, and you didn't know how to refuse. The cheek tasted of rotting, of poison flowers. You went to the toilet to spit. Watched her eyes close and mouth open, but didn't stick around to watch the rest.

You were in a room in Ohio, hundreds of miles away with nothing but some bags of clothes, stretched flat and burning holes on a moldy mattress, when Mom called to give you the news, real matter-of-fact. Like reporting about the weather or the price of milk. Still, there was no right way to ask her—to send the leftover meds in the mail. But you did. *Figure no sense them going to waste.* And she did. You didn't spend long considering what this said about you, as a person. As people. And why would you? Death is hard enough.

Down the Way

You've been kicked out of school so many times they finally say don't come back. Now you stay down the way with a dozen other fools in a graffitied row house where the landlord knocks dollars off the rent in exchange for "fixing up the place."

You paint a few walls, strip some hardwood. The toilet's been busted for weeks, but when you gotta go, you gotta go, so you burn incense, dull your senses with malt liquor and so much smoke.

There's a Fry Daddy in the kitchen, oil so old it's black in the vat, but man can you cook. Living on potatoes and loaves of discount bread your mom drops off when she hasn't seen your face in a while.

You still come around home now and then, to get a real shower and feel some real heat, to sleep in a bed, which she keeps for you because no matter what you're always her baby.

I'm good, you tell her. Getting along fine.

She asks you about that shooting, the drive-by on Ohio Avenue. Did you hear about it?

What you don't tell her: it happened right outside your door. The little girl playing in the yard across the street when it all went down didn't get hit, no one got hit, but you know how she frets. Instead of telling her the sun was shining, shafts of October light slanting through the screen door, that first you heard the *Pop! Pop!* sound so familiar you hardly took notice, and then the squealing rubber and the car, long Lincoln or Caprice, rounding the corner and up the hill—instead of that you say, *Naw, that's news to me.*

Three Photographs of the Mother

1.

The mother as conqueror, straight-legged, atop a stone hearth, stretching skyward, one hand pressed to a still-young womb, inching toward a still-strong heart. Eyes stare forward. Or is it down? Wild growth roves, fences contain the wild spaces.

She is above it all but grasping, something higher than the highest trees, the ones whose hard arms will be always reaching, to block her light and pin her down.

2.

The mother as prisoner, prim and proper, behind bars. Mid-century suburbia.

Look in the mirror—is that a flaw or something else, the echo of another her calling back, to warn of what's coming: kids, sickness, sets of broken vows? Long hours and longer days and bones bruised beneath their weight. Perhaps she's saying, *Lift your feet girl. Make that chair your safe haven, and stay forever. Hurry while there's still time.*

The mottled carpet teems beneath her, and she is the last vestige, a past turned black, on the surface of an ageing brain.

3.

The mother as young woman, ol' lady, departed, breaking state lines in a runaway straddle, hopped up and hopping on the first two wheels that put it at her back. Leathered and free for a too short stretch, smile a windblown curve as the rugged rumble slices the heat of open air.

Fast Eddie liked to play with fire, she will say in some far away future, tired but wistful, and you will think, Just another name that could have been Daddy. *Odie who had the habit and was always dying. Mad Jack who could chew through a beer can.* Hard to say, when they shared so much love.

But for now there's never no *Where to next*? And it don't matter— 'cause she'll ride it to the end of the line.

Face to Face

After years of putting it off, you sit down with her to go over the details, the papers and forms and phone numbers, for not if but when.

And now, as she runs through what to do, you feel that old wall going up, the frustration at her constant digressions, the same ones you've inherited, which prevent you from getting to the point.

Just what's important, you say. *Just what I need to know. You're complicating things. It's too much to remember.*

You leave the room to get a drink, come back as she's putting the folder back in the drawer.

So is that everything? It's not, but she says it is. For now.

You want to stay with her, just sit and be with her, but you also want to leave because the air has grown too heavy and you have things to do. Places to be.

Outside it's spring, but cold. There's snow. You forget your gloves on her table. Later, when you realize this, you'll wonder if you did it on purpose, just so she'd call to tell you.

Elegy for an Uncle (?)

He was always the one you took after, even when you were just a little shit who'd only visit in the summers, reveling in Grandma's material excess and how she'd spoil you kids rotten, while your mom stayed back in Ohio, in her own way reveling that she had one less mouth to feed for a couple months.

He lived in the basement with the pool table and the bar, the tacky wood paneling and rusty shag. Man, that was the place. That's where you learned to emulate a way of living. It got into your fibers, probably. Impossible to get out.

He took you with him and his girlfriend down to Milwaukee in his pickup truck, and on the way down let you shift and gave you your first taste of alcohol: the bottom third of a Bartles and Jaymes wine cooler. Strawberry. Like a revelation on your tongue.

When he got arrested on the lakefront—open container, public intoxication, drunk and disorderly, something in the neighborhood, anyway—the girlfriend, curly brunette hair and stonewashed jeans, thin T-shirt the only thing between her mature flesh and your accelerated six-year-old desires, kept you in her care and you watched as the car drove off with him in the backseat, his face a half-and-half of guilt and something else.

And there was the time he bet you five dollars he could swallow a live minnow and puke it back up whole and wriggling. You were maybe seven or eight at the time. He did it, and you were too young to know not to take the bet because where the hell were you going to get five bucks? So to impress him you swallowed one, too, but couldn't muster the guts to finish the trick, and even now, when you think about it, you can swear you feel it swimming around in there just behind your belly button.

That was the same summer you went to Florida, the time just the two of you went "cruisin'" along the beach in Grandma's truck with Pink Floyd cranked to a bone rattle, and he taught you how to hang your wrist over the steering wheel and "check out babes" while a fresh-cracked Budweiser sweats between your legs.

But he could be scary. Little guy with a ten-foot temper, ready to take on the biggest sonofabitch in the room, even when it was only himself standing in his underwear in the parking lot of some Louisville motel while you were on our way back from Disney World, you and your little cousin watching as he screamed at the night and Grandma pleaded in her gravelly voice for him to *Jesus Christ please come back inside.*

He'd get that look in his brown eyes and you'd just know one had checked out and another had checked in. A look someone close to you not long ago described during one of those next-day salvage missions where debris was all you could retrieve from the previous night, before the lights went out.

But he always remembered to call on your birthday, on Christmas, even when he was locked up in the joint.

Twenty years later and you'd bring out the worst in each other. He'd share his meds and you'd do weird things like move the TV or rearrange the furniture in your sleep. You'd deny doing it but suspect it was you and vow never to mix brandy and Vicodin and Rozerum again, because no matter how much fun it might be to hang out at a bus stop with Abe Lincoln and a deep sea diver like in the commercial, there's just too much of the wrong kind of potential there.

Lacking control in life, when awake, is one thing.

By then you knew he was dying, you all did, he had been for years. Nothing if not tenacious. The stalwart will of high tragedy housed in skid row architecture. But no one would take his calls.

And the thing is this: You think of your father's eyes—the ice blue of an arctic canine. Mom's green like soft moss. It's known to happen, yet you can't help but wonder, as you sort through what's been handed down, maybe your brown eyes aren't so special, after all.

Always Been a Rocket

Always been a rocket racing there, nowhere from nowhere if they're to be believed—only if they are. First hands inch at a tick to beer-thirty for dry tongues thirsty and barking dogs at the end of a long strain. Then the cut and skid to round a blind corner. And somewhere in the after black, the tumble, a snap flash to a cheek chewed raw, a flooded synapse for the broke and born ready. The flypaper summer blooming with open sores and sweaty crooks, dressed in schemes, nodding in the shade, tossing up in the running gutters, the dirty cottons and shots bleached clean and a city baritone asphyxiated, breath between words that catch in the throat of a kid whose can-do goes code blue in the upstairs room. And dying's not real cool. Smack to resuscitate. Don't want no bodies laid out, and don't need no ghosts hanging round if people ever gonna heal.

Where You Might Have Been When They Took Their Last Breaths

...and one morning the bonfires
leapt from the earth
devouring beings...

> – **Pablo Neruda**, *I Explain a Few Things*

Hey, Herbie said, Tony, can you fly?
But Tony couldn't fly—Tony died.

> – **The Jim Carroll Band**, *People Who Died*

You think: *Where was I when all these dead were dying, dropping off and piling up?*

Andy C. you knew since sporting chains in junior high. Slit the back of a Fentanyl patch to get at the inside. Time released all at once. Maybe you were tapping after snapping a vial, copped from a girl whose guy got slick, swiped some boxes from a truck. Around the time the towers came down, because you were still living in The Bricks, and despite the nights' new elevations you'd only begun to get the taste.

Amanda K. and Josh P., lingering from way back, each in a car and shouldn't have been. You down in some city, blacking out and tripping through windows, waking up swollen and scarred, getting a dollar any way you could to keep it going.

Carrie with the lip ring and razorblade grin, who told you once, while you were getting right at the kitchen table, her mom disowned her because she liked girls and dope, said, *because the devil done got hold of me by the ankle.* Maybe while she choked in that upstairs room you and your girl were sticking up your dealer with a steak knife or stripping seals from CD cases to unload up the road, after a three-for-twenty or a single bag.

Fawzaan, always falling out, behind the wheel at a four-way stop, in a corner, on a couch—couldn't come back from the last one. Joey B. with the busted teeth, maybe laid flat while you were towing cars on a quick lick to that shady ass scrapyard across town, or reviving Kyle in the bathroom, smacking around his naked lank, splashing him with cold water—*Don't you fuckin' die in my house*—getting him to suck some air, waiting to see he'd come out of it crying like a child so you could leave him there, sheet-wrapped and wet while you snatched the last of his stash. Didn't even think, *It could be bad batch*, before ducking to the bedroom, taking the shot that almost took him down.

That kid Kurt you turned on first so you could dip in. *Where was I*, you think, *when he turned up face down by a wife who never knew the truth*? Maybe with your girl, the one who worked for the phone-sex line, trading hot words and heavy breath in a back seat for a few balloons, while you hit up front and felt numb.

And how many others, picked off while you faked interest in pictures of your friend's friend's cat, distraction while he emptied the medicine cabinet, crotching a bag of rigs and a month's supply of the morphine that helped her cope with the cancer, killing her, you in your own way dying.

But you'd go on living and wonder why. Jesse and Steve and Tami J. never could get a grip but you somehow could. And you still wonder and can't take the worn out platitudes in the rooms, about God's divine hand. *He wasn't done with you yet*—as if the rest were just expendable. *He's got other plans for you*—as if their purpose had been served, time used up. The nerve it takes to say such things, and to believe them.

Danielle, who was always Danni. You knew her from a damn-near baby. Got so strung out she strung herself up in a closet far away from home, fields stretched out around her. And Donnie, whom you only met once but whose light was among the brightest, taken out like a heel-snuffed ember. Matt, who died on Christmas in a parking lot.

Aunt Dee-Dee had a whole life, kids, was a wife, and then traded it all for a fast slide down a slim glass pipe, then some kind of cocktail, keeping her sleeping when she should have woke up. Maybe when you were looting your in-laws—jewelry, antiques, whatever you could hawk for a South Side rock. Or by then sitting on your rack down on the compound, that joint surrounded by fences and hills, bitting, flexing, waiting to ride out. Paying that debt that would never be paid.

He works in mysterious ways, they tell you. Robbie and Katie and Crazy Ray. They say, *It's for Him to understand and us to trust.* Lance and Adam. *Some aren't meant for this world.* Your man Taz and Christina from the Heights. *They're in a better place.* You let the words, so many words, come at you. You let them land and roll off. Nikki. Denis. Eddie T.

You think: *All gone.*

And I'm still here.

So Fast, So Close

1.

Your mother tells you about emancipation, a way for you to be on your own, since it's what you want. Think about how maybe it's best for you both. Just sign on the line. Only once you do, you can't turn back. Can't return to wrist slaps and second chances.

2.

The Petra station doesn't card and lets you run a tab. And why not? You're steady and they know where you live, tell you so when you say, *Toss it on what I owe you.* They show you the shotgun, and you know the deal. Nothing subtle, just what it is.

You come in to cash a check, settle up and start over. Had some work, a friend of a friend knew a guy. Enough to get square.

Back at the house one of your roommates is in the driveway talking to some sketchy looking dude you've never seen.

You're about twenty ounces down then flat on your back in an upstairs room staring into a pistol's cold pupil. Everyone's on the floor. Don't even know how many there are because you're not about to move a muscle to count.

Then it goes from bad to full-on ugly when they take the girls right there—nothing you can do but listen to the sounds of it.

You know it's over when someone says, *You seen our faces, now you gotta die.*

They crack jokes and leave down the back stairs.

You read about it in the paper, in the mall of all places, looking at words that are supposed to tell what happened while all around you people move in and out of stores, safe and flush and miles away.

You console yourself with the dubious truth that if you'd have acted lives would have been lost. You'd be gone.

One day you'll write about it in fragments and failed metaphors. Trying to make it mean something.

But for now you move on.

You get by.

It's what you do.

3.

And this is where you see her first, twirling a mad mezcal dervish in the damp grass. Long skirt and bare arms.

But it really begins when she lays her feet, crossed at the ankles, casual as slow honey in your lap.

You can't keep your hands off each other after that. Fuck in the water and in the trees, on table tops. Washing machines. Every cliché. Fuck because Love could take more than either of you've got to give.

4.

Talking books and music and other tastes and tasting each other on the floor of your friend's apartment as the early morning blue bleeds through an empty bum-jug of cheap Sangria.

You make her coffee and share the last cigarette, which marks a great transition.

Let's not call it a thing, she says.

No, you agree. *Not a thing.*

But neither of you are stupid enough to believe it.

5.

You have a scare and tell yourself, *I would have done right, would have stepped up.*

And then again to call your bluff.

6.

Five days old and he lies in a blindfold under UV lights. Jaundice. Head coned from the vacuum.

They give you a special blanket to wrap him in when he needs to nurse. But the light is what he needs, and the blanket—it just doesn't seem strong enough so you put him back under the bulb.

They prick his heel to test his blood, bilirubin, and he cries, lies unclothed beneath the light. And he cries. All you want is to pick him up and let him see your face. But he needs the light.

You need the light.

And just like that it all comes back in blinding flashes, all those lows and close calls, and you fear for your child because he is *your* child.

Then the questions spin from one another, from images of all that could go wrong in these first days and the days that follow and on and on until forever comes to a stalling halt. They weave this picture of a life so fiercely sought and fought for, but it knots you up because it's not just yours anymore.

It's yours.

3

Father and Sons

This Is Why You Need Them

for Spencer

You've got this thing with names. Plants, rocks, native species.
Concrete details have become a favorite pastime.

Vehicles, clouds, chemical compounds.

You file away names in no particular order but know right where they
are when you need them. And you will. Need them.

Architecture, muscles, functions.

You pass names on to the little boy beside you at every turn. Holding
him up to the pull-up bar in the bathroom doorway of a thirty-year
mortgage, a pale blue neo-colonial, you say, *These are your lats, from
the Latin, meaning Latisimus Dorsi. And these, your traps, your
rhomboids. All work together in scapular adduction and internal
rotation.* You say, *Your Biceps Brachii are here, but we just call them
pythons or guns.*

And when you take him to the park: *This here is goldenrod, which
looks a bit like horseweed before it blooms in late summer.*

Pokeberry, Pin Oak, Queen Anne's Lace.

Sometimes you quiz him, just for grins. You say, *What's this called?*

Tell me, he says. *Tell me tell me.*

You tell him. Everything you know.

Because even though the spot of blood on your pillow was likely just dry sinuses (epistaxis) or a scratched eardrum (otorragia), you never know, so you point it all out—the custom Ford Fairlane, the thin wisp of cirrus, the course of his August constellation—hoping he'll remember you.

The curve of your jaw in a gothic arch.

Your hand waving him on in a verge of bobbing foxtail.

How Does a Man Prepare?

How does a man prepare himself for the inevitable interrogation?
How does he determine his eventual reply?

The day will arrive when that smaller version of me will upturn his
hungry eyes, asking in eager tones of countless things.
But as his need to know it all grows, from innocuous inquiry to
existential tension, will I have the range to face him?

Do I dare delude by telling him his kind is brought by birds, and
thunder is God bowling a perfect game?
Or when he looks to the sky and asks, *Why blue*? do I wax elemental,
watching his eyes glaze over as I talk of the affinity of certain
molecules for certain hues, wavelengths, and refracted light?

Even questions that *have* answers require some strategy; to be
forthright takes forethought when molding a mind.

But what of God?
What of dreams and time and dying?
What of those heavy weights that have pressed down on so many
waking hours?

To him I will be the first source of knowing, for finding his way.

How does a man prepare himself?
How does he take care not to weaken the child's faith, his belief that
Father will guide him?

Would I be better armed for the barrage if, as a smaller me, I'd had a
bigger me instead of empty space?
Would I be able to satisfy the why's and what's?
Would I have access to the winning explanation?

I know no other story that would leave me more equipped.

So, how does a man prepare himself for the moment when he must starve those hungry eyes, upturned in anticipation, and say, *Son, I do not know*?

Part of What We Pass down Is Silence

after William Greenway

We cross the locked gate
and I say, *We used to come here
when I was young.* Show him the
painted names claiming space
on steel girders, more immortal than
we'd ever be. He's four, so I keep
much to myself: how we'd drive reckless, sometimes wrecking,
out in the country where the dark was different, darker,
would walk on a dare the slim length of rusted beams,
fearless on pilfered wine, or terrified
but afraid to admit it.

That decades-gone summer
I'd come back to my mom's apartment,
upstairs from the old Dutchman
who wore brimmed trilbies and tweed coats
and stank of sweet tobacco, back from school
or scrubbing dishes at the Point Tavern,
under-the-table wages without a permit. Money to be free
for a night or two. And there they'd be waiting—
Marcus and Dave and some kid from the projects
we called Diaper Dan because he looked so young,
though I was the youngest.

The summer of shared shoes, of taking turns.
Didn't matter where we'd been
because we'd all been there.
We knew what it meant to be poor.
The summer she told us to stay inside her
because she'd had her tubes tied—

Don't need no more mouths to feed, her mother had told her.
So we howled our adolescent madness and waited
our chance to hold and be held,
because we knew what it was like
to need to be loved.

I want him to know it's okay to be afraid,
that nothing's so important in those fast moments,
besides living, that it needs to be proved. That there's being brave
and being fooled, despite surviving.
Some of us.
I want to say the ones we keep close are rarely those who were closest,
in times preserved because they were always on the cusp of ending.
But what sorts of things are these to give a child?
We'd come here to hear the ghosts, I say. The sun is out, and birds.
I race him back to the car, his laughter lifting, drifting through the
trees,
out there where we left our own, where it might well live forever.

When at Last the World

He's finally reached that age now
at which I know he'll start to
remember, slivers and flashes,
as if through driving rain,
as I do the days walking
the playground's perimeter,
where older boys sunk stones
through chain nets, while I plucked
flat packs of Marlboros from the
guttered trash and raised them to
my lips like a real man shaking one free,
and of pressing pennies into copper
petals on steel rails when the freights
still came, of a new city and never less
than a little fear to keep me taut and
humming like a wound wire,
the growing gap where a home should be,
the trying, always, to believe in something,
anything, real.
So I wonder, at times like this,
what his will be.
Where and when will be
his ghosts.

Visitation

Back then, weekends were for fishing. Fishing was what Dad would have done, if he could, all day every day till the sun went down. Down by the willow tree or out on the pier, that long jut of concrete in the cold north water. Water there washed up the sides like a pulse or a hissing breath. Breath itself a net gathering in the reek of dead fish, damp air, and the hoppy froth of popped bottles. Bottles were how they held their lines. Lines cast and set to drift while portable radios chattered and sang all along the narrow ledge and men sat on upturned buckets sucking suds, listening for that bite, the clank of a bottle tipping over.

Over the far away edge, out there, lost in the still-dark morning, was where the sun lurked, behind the night but right before us. Us—a boy, his old man, the huddles of men denying Time's dying with just another and another and another casting out.

Out there, though, it was just us two in spite of it all. All that had come to pass before and beyond my knowing. Knowing that for just that short time, I was his son again. Again I bit down on this thing with no understanding. Understanding would come later. Later on the steps maybe, little by little, each time he dropped me at the door, until the thrumming in my center reached the right key, moved me to the cusp of a feeling unwieldy in its opposing motions, how it left me needing each extreme, taking it in and making it mine. Mine was the sadness and joy of leaving, the sadness and joy of coming back.

Early Riser

I should have known
it would end up the way it did

—each do-over less successful
than the last—

because all along he was an early riser,
and though I looked forward

to those cold mornings on the pier
or under the shade of the willow tree

where I hooked my first fish,
a fat brown trout (how proud he was!),

inside my clock was set
to noon.

We tried again
all those years later,

as if the week between our times
had only been put on pause,

but I left again,
now of my own accord,

for what reason
but that I was young

and needed to be everywhere
but where I was?

And not so long ago,
mornings I rose against my nature

to shovel sand and pour concrete
because *a man's got to make a livin*,

to pay the bills if nothing else,
I'd remember that besides our anger

we're nothing alike,
and I'd wonder if,

had I stayed the first time,
maybe we would be.

What She Kept, What She Carried

She never said a bad word about you
till I was grown:
how she'd borrow money from Granny Grace
for diapers and formula because you just
had to have that new rod and reel.
That time you broke her nose.
Or when you knocked her down to the sidewalk
outside the Golden Arches and tried
to take me away.
When those two big women ran you off
as she lay on top of me, shushing and singing
so I wouldn't be scared.
The world's horrific enough without fearing
the ones you love,
the ones you miss when you can't reach them.

I suppose it makes sense—
her propensity for damaged men,
damaged as she was
by them,
and by her own mother,
who raised her to believe she deserved no better.

On Bestowing an Unwieldy Inheritance

If I could ask
one thing
it would be
that he bear
the best of me
and not the rest,
for him to be
spared,
and should his
doubts or sorrows
grow too unruly,
his rage,
may he
tame them,
may he know
when to steel
and when to yield
against their
weight.

Spirits of Ochre

They said we had *journeyed together*
in another life, but not as father and son, as brothers,
somewhere *warm and relatively near the ocean.*
Our father was a village blacksmith, and I wonder
if the numbness in my hands is from stoking the forge
and striking iron. Just how far memory can travel.
Through time and space and soft skin.
Porous bones, helix of our genes.
Inside out or outside in.

One of us would someday succeed him, we knew,
but didn't know who because *both were dreamers.*
We *dreamt of being by the sea,* and it was only after
one of us fell in love that we finally decided,
though it wasn't clear which was which.
He or I *chose to stay,* while he or I went forth
in pursuit of dreams.

He was much too young, no age to ask if he remembered,
and I'm too old now, hands callused
not from hammer and anvil
but gripping hatched steel to keep strong.
And tonight he sleeps, I hope still dreaming.

When he wakes, perhaps I'll raise the question:
Do you remember when we were brothers?
And if he loved, or what the dream was.
What it looked like.
If he ever reached it.

We Were in the Sun

It's like the time he discovered his mouth: his sounding out, his bi-labial blurbs, tongue across cut gums and clicking the ridge, his hinging jaw and *yaw yaws* endowing vowels with new yet primal music, twisting syllables, articulations caught in the throat, sorting and tugging and putting together with deep-chest pressure a voice. One that would and will undo silence, break down walls, carry on the echo of our blood. And now the words are his own, and the memories he speaks, wrestled from the air, pinned with a gesture, transformed. So much would escape us if not for the moorings of the senses, and of our children, who come to us with our histories held in their hands like artifacts unearthed from the garden—a rock, an empty shell, a shard of broken glass. He reminds me of the time *we were in the sun*, as if he already knows we are just dust settled and pressed into these forms after eons adrift in the wake of a snuffed out star. He tells me, as he weaves through the grass and climbs among the dappling branches, *I'm trying to run away from my shadow*, as if he already knows it's how we spend so much of our lives, resisting teeth—gravity, the darkness nipping at our heels. And I wonder what else he knows. He laughs and says, *Do you wanna see into a mirror?* I say yes. He says, *Then look inside my eyes.*

Merrill, WI

Fifteen years, close to thirty if you count
each absence, and a 700-mile rift
between us. All those times wondering
if you wondered why, or if you simply cast
the question from your mind like you
cast so many weighted lines,
no real expectation of hooking the big one,
but quietly hoping.

And now another spill into that past
I thought I'd only touch again in memory
and sleep.

If not for this small boy, descended from us,
to shield us from the heavy air awaiting,
the weight of missing years and lost moments,
would I have done this sooner?

Of course, there's no knowing now,
with him here behind me, and you there,
at the end of this long road we travel
to meet you.

Acknowledgments

———————————— ♦ ————————————

Special thanks are owed to Steven Reese for his years of guidance and insight, and for his astute input on this manuscript. To Mary Biddinger for offering advice and resources when I came calling. To Mindi Kirchner and Sarah Burnett for their feedback and friendship. To William Greenway, whose poetry I discovered late, but that served as a great inspiration in the writing of the final section of this book. To Robert Vaughan and Samuel J. Fox for their kindness and support. To Rusty Barnes for creating a space for some of these poems to take shape. To Steve Lambert and Ralph Pennel for their gracious reviews. To Stephen J. Golds and the gang at Close to the Bone Publishing for championing my work and sharing it with others—the writing community is lucky to have you on our side. To James A. Hegyi for being the best uncle a black sheep kid could ever have (R.I.P.). To Tom and Sandi Muir for welcoming me into the family and putting up with me all these years—I know it hasn't always been easy. To my mother and my wife, Rebecca, both of whom played enormous roles in the experiences from which many of these poems grew. To my daughter, Esmé Gabrielle, for being a bright light in this dark world. And finally, to my father and my son, Spencer Thomas. This one's for you.

Publication History

◆

Many thanks also go to the editors of the following journals, in which some of these poems originally appeared, sometimes in different form:

Anti-Heroin Chic: *Winnipeg, Street Kid's Guide to Coming up Aces in Columbus, Ohio,* and *So Fast, So Close.*

Jump: International Journal of Modern Poetry: *Kenora* and *Flagstaff.*

Live Nude Poems: *Missoula* and *Cheyenne.*

Switchblade Magazine: *Seattle* (section 1)

Defenestrationism.net Flash Suite Contest runner-up as *Disarticulated Life, Always that Child, The First Sign, 1988, Like Yesterday, No Grand Departure, Past, Present, Future, Water off a Broken Wing,* and *After the Hands.*

Gordon Square Review: *Before She Stopped Living.*

Kentucky Review: *Elegy for an Uncle* (?)

(b)OINK: *Where You Might Have Been When They Took Their Last Breaths.*

The Bookends Review: *This Is Why You Need Them*

Volney Road Review: *Part of What We Pass Down Is Silence*

Neologism Poetry Journal: *We Were in the Sun* (nominated for Best of the Net 2019)

About the Author

◆

William R. Soldan is a fiction writer and poet from the Ohio Rust Belt. He is the author of the short story collections, *In Just the Right Light* and *Lost in the Furrows*, as well as the forthcoming collection *Houses Burning and other Ruins* (Shotgun Honey, 2021), and the forthcoming novel, *Undone Valley* (Cowboy Jamboree Press, 2021). He currently resides in Youngstown, Ohio, with his wife and two children.